The Buddha's first noble truth, the truth of suffering arises from human difficulty in a nence of things. Everything changes, the b remains constant. Or as Ching-Yuen has it:

> We can hold back neither the coming of the flowers
> nor the downward rush of the stream;
> sooner or later, everything comes to its fruition.
> The rhythms are called by the Great Mother,
> the Heavenly Father.
> All the rest is but a dream;
> we need not disturb our sleeping. [*On Tao*, 5]

The second noble truth, the truth of the cause of suffering, which deals with desire and the futility of overweening ambition, is clearly recognized in the prelude to Ching-Yuen's text:

> Gain and renown are hindrances
> to students of the Way;
> they taint our purity of heart.
> Uncentered, how can we comprehend Tao?

As a highly skilled martial artist, Ching-Yuen brings the unwavering self-discipline of the martial adept to his approach of attaining, and maintaining, spiritual harmony amid the tossings of ordinary life. There is a frankness in his remarks concerning dharma practice that cuts through poetic or metaphysical chit-chat, and that echoes the training hall:

> Since ancient times, among all peoples
> virtue has embodied the Way,
> though true Tao has no shape
> and is discerned only as the fruitful path.
> But no more talk about it—right practice
> means aching limbs. [*On Enlightenment*, 3]

Right practice and right livelihood, cornerstones of the Buddha's eightfold path, again are embraced without contradiction:

Students of Tao must appreciate one thing:
Everyday, mindful practice.
When the mind is disciplined
then the Way can work for us.
Otherwise, all we do is talk of Tao:
everything is just words;
and the world will know us as its
one great fool. [*On Enlightenment*, 6]

There is something in all of this that has to do with living in the eternal moment, and, in a Buddhist sense, with treading lightly upon the earth. Whether we know it as the middle way, the water-course way, or simply the Way, what Ching-Yuen has to say will be familiar to those acquainted with the Tao-te Ching, the Confucian *Analects*, the writing of Shunryo Suzuki, or the poetry of such monkish bards as Han Shan, Basho, and Ryokan. As a teacher he borrows at will from the greats, restating and reworking what has gone before — and for the best of reasons: to inform, and to entertain, for there is poetry in his utterance that calls to mind the literary treasures of the Tang poets who have long enlivened Western appreciation of the Middle Kingdom.

Toward the end of his life, Ching-Yuen did attempt to establish a temple in Nanking, but given the calamitous upheavals of 1949 his efforts were not successful. Afterward he lived in Hong Kong, and from there journeyed to the United States where he lectured to Chinese communities. His discourses during this visit were re-counted by a disciple, Lu Hue-Ming, and they in fact constitute the frame of the text which follows.

Ching-Yuen died in San Francisco in the early 1960s. Surprisingly, other than his teachings that have been left to us, we know little of his personal history. What, though, do we know of Lao-tzu or Chuang-tzu other than that they were very wise old men?

Loy Ching-Yuen's book is about an approach to living simply and honestly in this world, and the reader will note the symbolism at-tributed over and over again to the heart as our center of con-

TRANSLATOR'S INTRODUCTION

sciousness, as the locus of real self. His directness and simplicity of transmission, with emphasis always on *practice*, rather than speech or ideals, offers something valuable for every student of the Way, particularly now as it finds and spreads roots in the West. The English title has been chosen for this reason; while it is close in meaning, it is not exactly that of the Chinese original, which, literally, is closer to "The Book of Rectifying Your Heart."

Prelude

Gain and renown are hindrances
to students of the Way;
they taint our purity of heart.
Uncentered, how can we comprehend Tao?

Purifying our self-direction,
our emotions, and behavior in all endeavors,
one grows in understanding of the Way.
But individual abilities vary
and the exalted Way has many different rules.
To students of Tao, this sincere forewarning:
Only with a clear, honest spirit can we begin meaningful learning.
With an unsullied heart we may even move the immortals.
Debasing the Way, not even heaven forgives us.

ON PURIFYING THE HEART

ᢒ 1.

Two methods enable us to rectify our heart:
The first is study,
enriching our mind through practice and discipline;
training, studying until an inner light begins to grow within.
This seed of consciousness, the sages teach, should be nourished
   and kept in silence.

The second is the cultivation of Virtue.
A sincere student discovers the workings of Tao by overcoming all
   manner of temptation.
Hordes of riches are outweighed in merit by a single word,
Virtue.

Cultivating goodness in the heart is like planting spring grass:
While its growth is imperceptible, day by day there is increase.
Evil in the heart is like the working of a rasp:
Daily we sense decrease through its honing.

With a proper heart we master the Way naturally.
Understanding its profundity we may use it effectively in our lives.
The key is discrimination between good and bad,
in loyalty without desire.

ᔥ 2.

The finest of moral integrities?
Sincerity. Square and true.
A sincere, tranquil heart is like a bright shining mirror,
uncontaminated by a single speck of dust.

Millions of secrets evolve from one similar source:
From roots, dust, emptiness.*
Therein lies the one principle:
Buddha-nature lives in a pure, empty heart.

*The six roots (eyes, ears, nose, tongue, body, mind) are the sensory organs which touch the external world. The six dusts are corresponding objects (sight, sound, smell, taste, touch, thought). The six realms of emptiness correspond to the above (empty mind, etc.).

THE BOOK OF THE HEART

⨳ 3.

The gates to the Way are manifold;
each is profound and effective.
But deepest and finer is the sky beyond the sky, that, understood,
    corresponds to the Tao of heaven.*
For the Way is vast and without favor
and the all-empty Tao is profound.
With an empty heart, its nature is easily learned,
though its power encompasses the cosmos.
With its wisdom one may discern life's great mysteries,
so that the heart may become pure as the throne of the immortals.

---

*In Chinese Buddhism desire is associated with the sixth sky, location of Xu Mi mountain, home of the god *Shi Tian,* who lives in its center. Xu Mi is surrounded by four peaks, each having its own eight skies. Desirelessness is equated with the thirty-third sky—"the sky beyond the sky."

ဆ 4.

Like muddy water our heart awaits cleansing;
turbid or clear, its nature is of our choosing.
Black or white, right or wrong—
these things come from the heart and its training:
Destiny is shadowed by the color of our intentions.

With prayers and a calm mind the Way can be understood
   and attained:
The roots of wisdom are heavenly endowed.
With Tao implanted in our heart,
we ourselves may become buddhas.

No use fretting over gold, beauty, or fame;
nurturing these, how can we calm our fluttering heart?
Non-attachment brings deep truth,
and a truthful nature brings immortality.
Empty your heart.
Sit quietly on a mat.
In meditation we become one with All;
Tao billows like the vapors in a mountain valley,
and its supernatural power wafts into our soul.

THE BOOK OF THE HEART

ᡠ 5.

We must do our best to purify our heart:
Hard work, steady practice, and a clear spirit are necessary.
Purity and emptiness are the elements of the heart-training
    method.
Mastering them is the natural route to Tao.

A heart free of desire is true emptiness:
No holding back, just drift with the untied clouds,
existence and non-existence are one and the same:
Embrace the void.
To the seeker, emptiness is All.

The universe overflows with spiritual treasure
yet it is empty and unsentimental.
In its nature there is justice.
Utterly impartial, the Way commands respect:
No greed, no evil; our heart is empowered with Tao.
No brightness, no darkness:
The view remains as it is.

On Purifying the Heart   7

CULTIVATING THE HEART

1.

Clouds and rain shroud the gateless gate;
frost and snow veil the winding road.
With contemplation and subtlety of spirit we discover Tao
and the secret of the Way grows within us.

Why is the root of wisdom so deep?
Because it must be planted in our lives.
Worries, doubts, illusions — cast them out forthrightly.
The road to the precious capital is not for the inattentive.

The book of Tao implants great wisdom but self-knowledge
   is individually different.
So it is said, "Plant melons, get melons;
plant beans, get beans."

᠗ 2.

When our senses are tempted, doubt arises easily in mind;
when emotions are not tempered, passion quickly seizes our
    physical being;
when the six realms of the senses are not at peace, our very soul
    is shaken:
Be healthily alert. Reject avarice and lust.

The wind bears no shape or shadow,
has no abode;
in meditation, be as the wind—
without image, without dwelling:
This is the wisdom of the heart.

3.

In the changing of the constellations
we study the criterion of the universe;
in the alternation of clouds and rain
we see clearly the harmony of nature.

Tao is a mysterious presence;
it eludes the sharpest tracker.
Acquiring knowledge of the Way
we must return to simple beginnings
that come naturally, like the rules of music.
As the mist lifts
and stars usher forth the moon,
we see the true path winds all around us.

ॐ 4.

Half-heartedness in things, an unsteady spirit
is an obstacle in one's study of Tao.
Willpower—determined effort in practice—
this is the key;
every element of motivation meshing in harmony.
In every undertaking,
be trim as the purposeful workings of the hand.

In practice, embrace the void;
let nature take the lead.
With the sword of wisdom one progresses dutifully upon the Way.

THE BOOK OF THE HEART

5.

In dead of winter
a stove of burning charcoal is bestowed
as earth and heaven spin,
yin and yang swirling ceaselessly,
light to dark and back again,
forming ch'i.

The drifting music of the evening flute,
the wax and wane of the moon—
with a glimmering of the stars our heart may change:
Relish these healing moments.

The sword of wisdom does not display its sharpness readily;
our mortal foolishness is quickly shattered by a single clever word;
in the empty mirror the teacher is met at last.

Chisel, sculpt—work until your inner light
is pure as apple jade;
this is the way of the buddhas.

⚘ 6.

Olives taste bitter at first,
sweet later.
So the matter of practice:
Hard work discovering the true Way.

Women of the pleasure quarter . . . ?
Ephemeral as rainbows, not nearly as glorious.
This world of artifice . . .
A change of wind, a change of make-up;
another gloss concealing yellow skin.

An inch of time is an inch of gold:
Treasure it.
Appreciate its fleeting nature;
misplaced gold is easily found,
misspent time is lost forever.

Like the yearning of a beauty locked away in a jeweled tower,
there's no end to human craving.
Overcome wanting mind.

ॐ 7.

Learning the Way means not wasting time;
diligent practice, over and over, is required.
We never know what we're after at first—
just an abstract idea.
Step by step, we get a handle on things,
we learn to bear all kinds of burden,
even worry.

When our heart is empty the light of Tao shines within us;
yet this radiance should not be displayed.
The sublime has all manner of power;
acknowledging this allows us to enlighten the lost.

A slim and willowy lady is what the gentleman sought,
but not all women are submissive.
In the end they walk their own different ways.
Clouds and mud divide our lonely boats.

Quiet emptiness,
drifting like clouds without direction:
Coming and going without hindrance.
This is the true Way.

Real power is empty, without image.
Like buddha-nature, its blessings are sublime:
No sound, no form, no color.

🕸 8.

A white lotus blooms in a green pond,
with a beautiful Buddha-image amid the petals.
Buddha-nature is like the lotus—
so clear and bright not even the thickest mud can stain it.

By a green jade lake—what a wonderful sight:
an old hermit fathoming Tao.
Aren't they the lucky ones; humble and still,
quietly humming the melodies of heaven?

A skilled sailor travels many seas;
a good field changes hands many times.
Chasing glamour and riches, we find clouds and smoke.
Instead, sit gracefully with a single stick of incense;
drift among the white clouds
wild as a river heron.

ON TAO

ஒ 1.

No counting chickens before they hatch;
forget promises or guarantees with the Way.
But diligent practice and cultivation of no-mind spirit is
    advantageous nevertheless,
bringing remarkable power to our disposal.

A raw pearl is a treasure but lacks luster;
polish it and how it shines!
Just so with ch'i:
Entering our heart, it resonates like crystal,
enjoining us with the sublime.

    No trace when it arrives
    No warning as it departs
    No color, no sound
    Formless, unfathomable as mist

Rivers and oceans,
oceans and rivers:
No matter their depth or flow
each shares the nature of the other.
Dealing with others, remember this:
be mindful as the compassionate sea.

ᘰ 2.

No time to lose worrying about enlightenment;
forget about ambition—hide your talent in the coalshed:
Let your wisdom speak for itself.

The power of the sword lies not in anger
but in its unsheathed beauty:
In potential.
The marvel of ch'i is that, internalized,
it radiates in flow like a golden shaft of light
anchoring our spirit
with the universe.

THE BOOK OF THE HEART

ஓ 3.

Life is a dream,
the years pass by like flowing waters.
Glamour and glory are transient as autumn smoke;
what tragedy—for with the sun set deeply in the west,
still there are those
lost among paths of disillusionment.

Our heart should be clear as ice.
Forget all the worldly nonsense.
Sit calmly, breathe quietly, heart bright and spotless as an
    empty mirror.
This is the path to the Buddha's table.

ᖂ 4.

The Way is just and can be savored by the virtuous:

  No nepotism
  No discrimination between rich and poor

With honesty and faith, all can be taught:
Tao saves us from catastrophe.

Some things should not be touched;
willowy things, bought and sold in the streets that feed our greed,
dim our heart and mind alike
issuing forth every kind of darkness.

The boundless Way is encompassed only by the heavens.
The Way is solemn,
our loyalty is proven only in the heart:
With perfect form that itself is spirit
we become one with the buddhas.

Among distant green mountains and clear, frothing streams
an old hermit, door ajar, gazes outward
contented as can be.
He practices Tao to understand the truth—
a poor, joyous man becoming buddha.

꧁ 5.

What labor we expend sorting out our mundane chores
   year after year.
But doing them without regret or tears,
without resistance,
that's the real secret of *wu wei**
like the mountain stream that flows unceasingly:
Elsewise, all we do goes for nought.

We can hold back neither the coming of the flowers
nor the downward rush of the stream;
sooner or later, everything comes to its fruition.
The rhythms are called by the Great Mother,
the Heavenly Father.
All the rest is but a dream;
we need not disturb our sleeping.

---

*Wu wei is action through non-action, letting things take their course.

🕉 6.

Keep a cool mind;
practicing the way of Tao is like meditating on the Milky Way:
Easy to get lost in the big picture.
Instead, hold the universe in your hands.

No shape, no form, no sound—
Without force of mind we attain the Way.
Cultivating the sublime requires patience,
discipline upon the road:
This is how the work gets done.

About human affairs and existence—
empty yourself of ambition concerning these.
Heaven and earth, flesh and power;
meld them into one body,
one consciousness of Tao.

ᏑᏋ 7.

With brilliant lights and fireworks
people joyously celebrate the Lantern Festival*
and a sparkling new opportunity begins.
Alas, time passes like a spring freshet
and one magic night becomes a flurry of years.

In the clamor of busy life
snatch moments to calm your heart.
These times, one's mind can truly appreciate Tao,
its resonance and power.
With uncluttered heart and emotion
we can mount the dais of the blessed,
and choose for ourselves among dukes and ministers.

Becoming a buddha means understanding Tao, its many riddles,
like the clouds that grow by happenstance
or the moon that waxes by itself.

The sun sets quickly on mountain lakes
and scholars, like beauty
grow old too fast.

When flowers wither and flutter, broken-stemmed,
who recalls their delicate fragrance?
Tempering our emotions we forge the iron bonds of the raft
    that will guide us
on our final journey across the bitter sea.

*On the evening of the fifteenth day of the first lunar month, Chinese celebrate
with fireworks and displays of hand-made lanterns.

ॐ 8.

Old truths are the greatest;
accept them as they have been passed down—
most of all, their abstract nature,
for understanding comes in time,
leading us to the buddha-land.

With birdsong and the fragrance of blossoms the sun rises;
above the eastern gate, a flawless azure sky.
Attaining the Way we are like the sun
dawning with roseate fire.

The chaste moon climbs high above the wall
illuminating our distractions.
Shine beyond us, goddess, treasure of the night.
Bathe us in the light of Tao.

Practice mindfully day and night.
Screen our impurities as they rise in mind,
in daily commerce.
With the sword of wisdom, sit in the middle palace
    between loss and gain.
The Way is emptiness
without thought, without concern.

9.

What perplexity, what confusion—
Oh, our human heart,
this world of puzzles.
What mishap awaits along every road?
What plots, disillusionments?
But Tao will never be lost:
An inquiring mind; faith in the Way—
there is salvation.

A small skiff makes its way upon the river
drifts past enormous mountains
crosses mighty seas.
How is it that such small things as boats
traverse the boundaries
dividing men from men?

With right inspiration
the seeker too drifts past trivial barriers
to live out life
in the groves of Taoyuan.*

No point in fretting over dark thoughts;
after nightfall, sunrise
when old folk take their leisure in red pavilions.
Open mind, open schedule
brings happiness.

*The legendary realm of peach blossoms and everlasting peace.

ᏽ 10.

Without desire, without distress
we keep to our empty heart.
The beauty of the Way is that there is no "way."

   No self
   No this, no that

Everything, everything is simply emptiness.

ON ENLIGHTENMENT

𝕊 1.

Desire that has no desire is the Way.
Tao is the balance of wanting
   and our not-wanting mind.

Travelers know steep cliffs mean a long, hard climb.
Just so with Tao:
No smooth roads without first a few ups and downs.

2.

One merciful thought on behalf of another brings harmony.
A kind and goodly nature brings us to the Way.
True attainment is dependent on our actions:
Talk without good deeds is a waste of time.

Ambition.
We want to scale the steepest cliffs to lofty heights.
But forget about ambition; get on with the work of climbing,
this is what the sages tell us.
Vinegar has its own sweetness.

Wisdom is real wealth:
its rays shine forth like supple gold.
Forge your skills till they too shine like treasure:
Then the knowing see power
in the corners of your smile.

3.

A truthful, unwanting heart forms the right foundation.
No nepotism—this forms the law.
Foundations based on principles are safe from danger;
with inner confidence we may embrace the abstract.

Cultivating goodness in the heart,
we are rewarded in kind with goodness vast as green meadows.
Since ancient times, among all peoples
Virtue has embodied the Way,
though true Tao has no shape
and is discerned only as the fruitful path.
But no more talk about it—right practice
means aching limbs.

Silence the tongue.
Sit still, notice the incense that envelops the entire room.
Practicing one's art dutifully,
positioning oneself to aid the flow of ch'i—
this is a practical way of savoring heaven.

෨ 4.

A late autumn evening,
moon obscured by occasional shadow;
spectral light illumines oddly formed clouds.
The grasses have faded,
leaves have fallen to ground.
Such moonlit ambiguity.
Where can we find similar abstract truth in humankind?

෨ 5.

To truly master the Way
we must pass through all life's hellish cycles;
at last, we reach the higher heights.
Only three things necessary for paradise after all:
endurance, alertness,
and a righteous heart.

All's one.
Green jade, blue ripples flecking the current.
Time flows past like water, singing,
"Don't say the hero is a young man:
Already he is white of hair."

ᏕᏕ 6.

Without contemplation
how can we become wise?
Following the Way, first we temper the mind.
This is how we comprehend the abstract.
Without knots or barriers in mind
we see and hear Tao easily,
reaping good harvest from our practice.

Students of Tao must appreciate one thing:
Every day, mindful practice.
When the mind is disciplined
then the Way can work for us.
Otherwise, all we do is talk of Tao;
everything is just words;
and the world will know us as its
one great fool.

‿ 7.

The Way carries from generation
to generation,
teaching goodness, Virtue,
bringing wisdom to the sage.
Hard to explain how it works;
like a golden proverb its nature is
exact
in tracing the path of Virtue.

∽ 8.

With a quiet heart it's good to practice Tao
exercising our power in the inner places,
the source of our knowledge.
Diligence fosters the effortless flow of ch'i
enjoins us with All,
omnipotent Tao,
self subsumed by non-self;
the pearl within the oyster.

ꙮ 9.

The roots of heaven and earth are found
in yin and yang.
Ch'i is born of the same marriage
of light and dark,
male and female.

The roots of Tao we find in *wu wei;*
both it and *you wei** are manifestations
of purest ch'i.
Mastering the Way we may use either with equal facility;
no need, though, in exerting undue force:
Non-action often serves our purpose just as well.

*The path of deliberate human action

⅏ 10.

Ah, midsummer!
Ripening fruits, rich vines, evening perfume,
with the waxing moon clear and full.
How the old scholars understood the transience
of these secluded moments.

The sage of Diamond Mountain asked,
"Who knows how to reach the thirty-third sky,
the sky above the sky?"
The Way is profound and difficult,
an abstract matter;
heaven lies within the deepest realms of the heart
in living things that drift like dreams
and end in a blink,
detaching the dust of Self at nightfall
in the ink of clouds.

Boiling up the soup of immortality takes hours on the stove,
like learning the Way: just one method—
practice diligently:
Heaven is within the grasp of all.

THE BOOK OF THE HEART

෨ 11.

An unspectacular life may be a garden rich in delight,
in queer paths, perfumed herbs, and marble cloisters.
"I live a life of no major accomplishments,"
said the oldest man alive.
High living is ephemeral, quick to change;
the light soon dims atop tower peaks.

With mindful practice
we may achieve no-mind,
the deepest secret of the Way.

Honing one's skill is the surest road to Tao;
like gaining Nothing from something
or something from Nothing.

Keep to your own counsel.
In the marketplace, be like the hazy drunkard;
forget about yin and yang.
Hide such knowledge in the cuffs of your sleeves;
those who know may pull it in or out as they wish, like
    an old magician.
Tao is the inexhaustible force;
it can be used at will.
Within its powers, the *bagua* and the five elements*
decide our lucky chance.

Bagua, or the "eight steps," are a series of trigrams drawn from the *I Ching*
representing changes in various transitional states. Their classification encompasses movement within compass points: family and abstract human relation-
ships, organic and sentient attributes, and so forth. The five elements—metal,
wood, water, fire, and earth—were held by the ancients to compose the phys-
ical universe; they are also used in explaining physiological and pathological
phenomena in traditional Chinese medicine, Taoism, and the martial arts.

꧁ 12.

Practice and practice to be faithful
the way a blacksmith forges iron,
hammer and hammer.
For truth and falsehood have no difference in time:
today, Prime Minister;
tomorrow, nothing.
Truly, true can be false;
false can be true.
And things are not always what they seem to be.

ᨒ 13.

Young girls yearn for pretty dresses;
summer flowers offer up their sweetest face.
The seeker wants another level of mind
and strives for it without distraction
like a grandmother shopping at market.

Once the light illuminates our confusion
the power of Tao germinates within us.
We see no-mind is equal to the majesty of kings.
Seek it as you would seek wealth and reputation;
work steady as the peasant farmers tending their
    crops every day—
this is the secret of Tao.

ॐ 14.

Consider the grandeur of wisdom,
real wisdom of the heart.
What else enobles us?
Invisibly it is passed from one generation to another,
the virtuous receive it without instruction,
without rhyme or pattern.
Slowly unveiling its key truths to others,
steadily, leisurely, these teachers walk on
to the buddha-land.

⬡ 15.

To know Tao
meditate
and still the mind.
Knowledge comes with perseverance.

The Way is neither full nor empty;
a modest and quiet nature understands this.
The empty vessel, the uncarved block;
nothing is more mysterious.

When enlightenment arrives
don't talk too much about it;
just live it in your own way.
With humility and depth, rewards come naturally.

16.

Enlightenment is hard to find;
the path isn't easy.
When we get it, no one sees or hears us.
But when it comes, another soul has unveiled the truth:
Excellence, faith, single-mindedness—
Click!

Rain and drizzle,
frost and icicles—
people are influenced by such forces,
are tempted by desire.
Stay alert! Students must understand
such enchantment.

Mountain after mountain, the path winds along its course
as crooked as a sheep's intestine.
Seeking Tao, one realizes why so few pass by the rugged trail.
And a wide, smooth road?
More difficult yet on the true path to Tao.

There's no end to study;
learning Tao, the modest talent must practice well.
A clear, persevering mind is the way to real empowerment,
to buddha-mind.

THE BOOK OF THE HEART

ॐ 17.

When there is no perceived difference
between square and circle,
light and dark in our minds,
we have attained the profound truth
of Tao.
Everything in heart should be as one:

    Emptiness
    Emptiness

ॐ 18.

Never forget the folly of greed;
we may as well swim against the current of
the Yellow River.

Training our inner self is like forging lead;
nine times a blacksmith turns his dipper in the flame.
Yin and yang, earth and fire
find their own harmony.
Precious metals and our inner pearl are waxed and
   chamoised with the pass of days.

When the mind is empty, blue flame licks the firebox.

ᔓ 19.

Sweet talk and pretty women are like honey,
but honey and wine are the ruin of heroes.
Take care to spare young green saplings
or the people's roots
will be shattered beyond measure.

A surfeit of flesh intoxicates the mind,
our will becomes disillusioned.
Nothing is accomplished by too much mucking about:
Overindulgence is the death of a strong foundation.

ॐ 20.

The fragrance of blossoms soon passes;
the ripeness of fruit is gone in a twinkling.
Our time in this world is so short,
better to avoid regret:
Miss no opportunity to savor the ineffable.

Like a golden beacon signaling on a moonless night,
Tao guides our passage through this transitory realm.
In moments of darkness and pain
remember all is cyclical.
Sit quietly behind your wooden door:
Spring will come again.

THE BOOK OF THE HEART

EVERYDAY PRACTICE

ᔰ 1.

After a storm at sea the sailor heads for home and quiet harbor.
Tossed by indecision
we must return our unsettled mind to the center:
Tao is within us all.
With many voices it has but one beautiful song;
many aspects but only one essence.
Though we are not bound, we are always connected.

Buddhahood is meditation;
with constant attentiveness our mind travels far:
into the highest hills and all over the world.
Elusive, delicate—we see the cosmos is empty
as well as full.
Nothing beyond, Nothing in hand,
Beauty, spirit, Tao—all one.

༄༅ 2.

The admired are truly beautiful
either with or without cosmetics.
Yet their lives too are graced with agitation.
Think peace of mind
rather than fame or wealth.
Casting off such worries, we bear a
lighter load.

ꙅꙅ 3.

Without words, we understand no-mind;
without shape, we understand true nature.
With relaxed mind, we grasp the meaning of Tao;
with the boundless Way, we understand truth.

‿ 4.

The great Way shines in our heart;
with wisdom we may understand its nature.
Comprehending the diverse keys of the profound and
glorious Tao,
we are as buddhas and will come to know the abode
of the immortals.